KIDS GET CODING

PROGRAMMING AWESOME APPS

Heather Lyons

Illustrations by Alex Westgate & Dan Crisp

Lerner Publications • Minneapolis

Contents

Children will need access to the Internet for most of the activities in this book. Parents or teachers should supervise Internet use and discuss online safety with children.

Getting Started

Hi! I'm Data Duck! I'm going to help you learn what apps are and how you can create your own.

In order to make an app, we need to understand how to write code. Writing code is what we do when we give a computer instructions. These instructions are saved within apps. They tell computers how to do all the different things we use apps for every day.

DATA DUCK

In this book, we will be using block-based code. These are instructions for computers that are stored in blocks. We can move and rearrange the blocks to write code. The blocks look like this:

```
when this character is clicked

ask "What's your
parrot's name?" and wait

say join (answer) "What a great name!"
```

There are lots of activities in the book for you to try out. There are also some online activities for you to practice. For the online activities, go to **www.blueshiftcoding.com/kidsgetcoding** and look for the activity with the page number from the book.

What Is an App?

"App" stands for *application*. An application is a program that tells your computer how to do a certain job. For example, a web browser is an app that shows you web pages on the Internet. We use other apps to play music and watch videos.

We can put apps on any type of computer: a laptop, a phone, a tablet, or even a watch! In this book, we're going to learn how to use code to make our own apps.

DATA DUCK

A computer is like a huge toolbox, and the apps that we put on it are the tools. We can use each tool to do a particular job. So adding a new app to our computer is like adding a new tool to our toolbox!

Top App

Think about your favorite app. What does it do? Write down three changes to the app that would make it even better.

What Do Apps Do?

From browsing the Internet and checking football scores to sending emails and listening to music, we can use apps for almost anything!

We use different kinds of apps for different kinds of things:

We use gaming apps to play and have fun.

If we want to practice math problems or find out about science, we can use an educational app.

To find out about the world around us or what the weather will be like, we can use information apps.

Communication apps help us to call or send messages to our friends.

We can watch a video or listen to a song on an entertainment app.

DATA DUCK

While some apps help us in everyday life, others can help make the world a better and safer place. There are apps that show people where safe drinking water can be found, and others that make it easy to contact the police in an emergency.

Using Apps

Data Duck and his mom are going to the museum. They have a phone with lots of apps. Can you help them choose the most useful app for each part of their trip?

1. Find out the museum's hours.
2. Look up bus times.
3. Pay for the bus.
4. Walk from the bus stop to the museum.
5. Take pictures of their favorite displays to show Grandma later.

Turn to page 23 to see the answers.

B: Camera app: takes pictures and stores them on your phone.

A: Bus app: tells you the schedules of all the buses.

D: Web browser: displays websites.

C: Map app: shows you a map of the area where you are.

E: Payment app: allows you to buy things without using cash.

Let's Plan an App!

Are you ready to build and code your first app? Before we start, we need to think about a few basic things. First, what will the app do, and second, who will use it?

As we know, apps are useful tools to help people do the things they need to do every day. So our app will show people how to take care of their pets.

The app could tell our user, Timmy, more about his pet. For example, it could say what the pet likes to eat and drink, and how often it needs to go to the vet.

Before we start coding our app, we need to think about all the things it should be able to do. Then we can use this information to create our app.

Careful Planning

When we build an app, we need to think of every single thing an app needs to be able to do. For example, when the app is showing Timmy how to feed his cat, it needs to tell him:

• when his cat needs to be fed
• what kind of food his cat needs

Think of at least two other things the app should tell or show Timmy, so he can give his cat food and drink.

The Design

Now that we have decided what our app does, we can start to think about what it will look like. This is the app's design.

Our app can show Timmy a lot of things about taking good care of his cat. So many things, in fact, that we need to think carefully about how we organize them all. This way Timmy will get the right information at the right time. One way to organize information in an app is to divide it into different screens. On the first screen, for example, Timmy might choose his pet. On the second one, he might find out how to groom his cat or how to play with it.

The Look

Once we know what all the functions of our app are, and which functions will appear on which screen, we can start to think about how each screen will look. Think about the first screen of our app. It will ask Timmy to choose the pet he has and wants help looking after. What will this screen look like?

What if...

We can use information from the world around us to help build our app. This will make it even more like real life!

For example, we could show that taking care of pets might be different depending on the time of year. If it's really warm outside, the app might tell Timmy how to take care of his cat in hot weather.

DATA DUCK

Our app can only know what the weather is like if it is connected to the Internet. Then, it can figure out where Timmy and his cat are and check the weather forecast for their area.

Cool Cat

We want our app to show Timmy how to take care of his cat in hot weather. Look at the steps below. Can you place them in the correct order to make sure the app works properly and gives the right instructions?

Turn to page 23 to see the answers.

Show picture of cat drinking water.

Show picture of hot, tired cat.

Receive message that the temperature is very high today.

Show picture of happy cat.

Show picture of water bowl.

Now go to **blueshiftcoding.com/kidsgetcoding** to try out the app!

Rewards

Let's imagine Timmy has done a great job of taking care of his cat. He has fed and groomed it well, and he knows when to take it to the vet.

How can we reward Timmy for doing so well? Maybe we can give him points every time he takes good care of his cat. The happier the cat is, the higher his score gets! This would make the app a little like a game too.

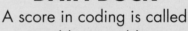

DATA DUCK
A score in coding is called a variable. Variables are like boxes where we store information that changes. The computer will keep track of the score for Timmy, so he doesn't have to!

Keeping Score

Data Duck has made a scoring system for our app.
Work out what the scores would be if:
• Timmy groomed his cat.
• Timmy fed his cat and changed its litter.

Turn to page 23 to see the answers.

```
when app starts being used

set score to 0
```

```
when I receive message "cat fed"

change score by +5
```

```
when I receive message
"cat litter changed"

change score by +2
```

```
when I receive message "cat groomed"
or "cat given toy"

change score by +3
```

Looking for Bugs

Our app is now designed and built! But before more people can use it, we need to test it to make sure everything works properly.

When apps have been coded, they are tested to make sure they are free from bugs. This is called debugging. A bug is an error in our app that stops it from working properly.

DATA DUCK
Coders always leave lots of time for testing their apps. Sometimes it takes longer to fix the bugs than it did to code the app in the first place!

Bug Hunt

When it is hot outside, the background image of the app should change to show a desert. Check these coding blocks and pick which one is correct.

Turn to page 23 to see the answers.

```
when I receive message "it's hot outside"

switch background to "desert"
```

```
when I receive message "it's hot outside"

switch background to "winter"
```

The app is supposed to tell Timmy that his cat has a nice name! Which block of code will tell him that his cat has a nice name, and which one will say nothing to Timmy?

Turn to page 23 to see the answers.

```
ask "What's your cat's name?" and wait

say join (answer) "What a great name!"
```

```
ask "What's your cat's name?" and wait

say join (answer) "..."
```

Publishing Your App

Once we have tested the app and made sure it doesn't have any bugs, we can publish it! Publishing an app means placing it on the Internet where it can be downloaded by users. But remember: never publish something on the Internet without the help of an adult.

Apps are often published in many versions. Each version is programmed in a different computer language. This is because each type of computer understands a different language. A phone, for example, might understand a very different language than a laptop would.

DATA DUCK
A hashtag—which looks like this: #—is used for keywords. For example, *#pets* means that "pets" is a keyword. Keywords are used to describe videos, games, and many other things on the Internet. So if someone is looking for an app about pets, and our app is labeled #pets, the person will be able to find it.

Labeling

When we publish our app, we must make sure it has the right keywords. This means that people searching for a pet app like ours will find it easily. Which keywords would be good for our app? Write down three that you think would be helpful.

Apps Help People!

Apps can help make the world a better place. We can make apps to solve all sorts of problems, big or small. And because a lot of people around the world can use computers, apps can also be used in many different countries. Let's think about some apps that could help people.

One idea might be to code an app that shows people how to recycle their garbage. The app could show them which materials can be recycled and how. It could also give tips on how to have less waste, and how to fix broken items or turn them into something new.

Another idea might be to code an app that tells people how to save water and energy at home. The app could tell them how much electricity they are saving when they turn off electrical items or how much water they are using when they do the dishes.

DATA DUCK

Apps don't need to have lots of amazing features. Some of the most popular apps are very basic. But even a simple app can be a very useful tool for people.

Over to You!

What problem would you like to solve? What kind of app could you make to help? Write down your ideas. You could even start planning and designing your app!

Extension Activities

Go to **blueshiftcoding.com/kidsgetcoding** for more fun activities and to practice:

- planning apps
- designing apps
- learning code
- debugging

Words to Remember

app: a computer program

browser: the program we use to access the World Wide Web

bug: a mistake in a computer program

code: the arrangement of instructions in a computer program

coder: a person who builds programs

debug: to find and remove bugs or errors in a computer program

function: a task that an app can carry out

Internet: a giant network of computers that are all connected together

variable: something that can be changed or adapted

Activity Answers

Page 7

1: D (web browser)
2: A (bus app)
3: E (payment app)
4: C (map app)
5: B (camera app)

Page 13

1. Receive message that the temperature is very high today.
2. Show picture of hot, tired cat.
3. Show picture of water bowl.
4. Show picture of cat drinking water.
5. Show picture of happy cat.

Page 15

If Timmy groomed his cat, the score would be 3. If Timmy fed his cat and changed its litter, the score would be 7—5 points for feeding, and 2 points for changing the cat litter.

Page 17

Coding block that will change the app background to desert:

```
when I receive message "it's hot outside"

        switch background to "desert"
```

Coding block that will mean the app tells Timmy his cat has a nice name:

```
        ask "What's your cat's name?" and wait

        say join (answer) "What a great name!"
```

Index

First American edition published in 2018 by Lerner Publishing Group, Inc.
First published in Great Britain in 2017 by Wayland, an imprint of Hachette Children's Group
Copyright © Hodder & Stoughton, 2017
Text copyright © Heather Lyons

Lerner Publications Company
A division of Lerner Publishing Group, Inc.
241 First Avenue North
Minneapolis, MN 55401 USA

For reading levels and more information, look up this title at www.lernerbooks.com.

Main body text set in Futura Std. Book 12/16. Typeface provided by Adobe Systems.

Library of Congress Cataloging-in-Publication Data
Names: Lyons, Heather (Heather K.), author. | Westgate, Alex, illustrator. | Crisp, Dan, illustrator. | Lyons, Heather (Heather K.). Kids get coding.
Title: Programming awesome apps / Heather Lyons ; illustrated by Alex Westgate and Dan Crisp.
Description: Minneapolis, MN : Lerner Publications, [2018] | Series: Kids get coding | Audience: Ages 6–10. | Audience: K to grade 3. | Includes bibliographical references and index.
Identifiers: LCCN 2016049275 (print) | LCCN 2016052665 (ebook) | ISBN 9781512439427 (lb : alk. paper) | ISBN 9781512455830 (pb : alk. paper) | ISBN 9781512450514 (eb pdf)
Subjects: LCSH: Computer programming—Juvenile literature. | Cell phones—Programming—Juvenile literature.
Classification: LCC QA76.6 .L8856 2018 (print) | LCC QA76.6 (ebook) | DDC 005.1—dc23

LC record available at https://lccn.loc.gov/2016049275

Printed in China

ML NOV 2017